THE HERD IN WORDS

Karen Kellock Ph.D.

Manual for Superior Men

This is a complete theory based on Einstein physics, Political Psychology, Systems Theory and Archetypal Psychiatry.

FORMULA

All success attraction
All disease obstruction
All recovery elimination

You must fast on all three

OBSTRUCTIONS:

People
Habit
Food

THE HERD IN WORDS

False kings collude together against God's men and women. Expect it: smear campaigns, gossipin'.   The human python is social hypnotism and it's all we've known in human society from the beginning.   People are cruel, they keep you down. Haters gotta hate something, it keeps their blood flowin'.   The bottom line rule: just extract yourself from fools.   We swim in muddy waters so we get stuff on us but it recedes with maturity then we just forget it.

OVERCOMING THE HERD

FEARING THEIR ANGRY FACES
ELIMINATION IS RECOVERY
DOGMATIC IMPERATIVES: "YOU MUST"
MARXISM SAYS: MEN ARE OPPRESSORS
DIVORCED MEN AND SUICIDE
LIBERALS FEEL SUPERIOR
LIMERENCE
ARE YOU LIMERENCED?
THEIR ATTACKS ARE BUMMERS
THE CONFIDENT NARC IS FRAGILE
THE CURE IS GRATITUDE
BREADCRUMB RELATIONSHIPS
REFUGEES FROM DYSFUNCTION
TAKE CONTROL FOR TRUE SELF
WE ARE BORN SOVEREIGN
NOT ABOUT RACISM BUT POWER
THE END

OVERCOMING THE HERD

FEARING THEIR ANGRY FACES

I feared when I saw their angry faces approaching my house intending to even things up.

He's so into himself it's flashy and exciting but then the lack of relating is so dam disappointing.

Stop making excuses for disordered people. They are dangerous for you, unpredictable and evil.

Don't go there if it causes anxiety and fear. Don't run thru past events during the treason years.

You still shudder at what you went thru at the hands of your enemies. Try to curb thoughts like these.

The events were dark and bizarre: part of the season of treason when everything was weird.

ELIMINATION IS RECOVERY

Getting rid of stuff is more important than acquiring. It's a clearing without accumulation.

You acting dignified or independent threatens the superiority of the tyrant who owns that.

His own citizens are enemies while foreigners offer no opposition so he says "come on in".

FBI cannot be revamped: must debunk to reconstruct for they came after President Trump!

OVERCOME THE HERD

God has plans to prosper us, He said it. Every path has low points, expect it. It toughens: endure it.

They ALL knew the criminal abuse of power even in the Obama days. Every dam one of em ok.

Don't worry about a dry period. Those days are gone, this is just the calm before the storm kid.

DOGMATIC IMPERATIVES: "YOU MUST"

Cruel, sadistic, talks in imperatives: "you MUST". Think back: who does he remind you of?

Turn everything around that he says: putting down appearance with such biting cruelty of all gals.

It wasn't that it hurt but it put me in a constant state of anxiety and maladapted to life [cursed].

Things are so dire and no one knows about it. News is an arm of Biden's dems who censor it.

All I do is look at the view, it's what I do. From that comes eternal visions and insights too.

When all your high school friends are dead groupthink takes over making you think you're next.

Once on the begging end you're a better leader cuz you now have empathy and can judge therein.

MARXISM SAYS: MEN ARE OPPRESSORS

Men are the oppressor; women are the victims and the victims rule: what happens next is cruel.

Porn: They go there once, it all lines up on the right, click-click and they're in trouble with the wife.

OVERCOME THE HERD

I have great empathy for men because we were both persecuted by women, isn't that amazin'

When we finally see how deep, multidimensional and pithy everything is it brings tears to our eyes.

It's our natural tendency to fight back. To do them in [vindicate] but all we can do is pray and wait.

Women fight by getting on the horn either "inquiring" or simply killing your reputation darling.

DIVORCED MEN AND SUICIDE

Nine times more divorced men than women commit suicide. Unreported fact: men suffer/cry.

Men are an oppressed class. Little boys are blamed for all bad deeds of all men from the past.

The "male feminists" turn out to be sadists. Any reversal of truth for approval is foolish.

The suicide rate of divorced men is nine times more than divorced women: they SUFFER man.

If he won't take responsibility for his downer effect on your goals then you gotta do the clearing.

"If the energy's right/not right"... Where is this energy, vibrations or light stuff in the bible? Aye

I want money cuz I want sovereignty if life turns on me. Looking "up" to people for support is nasty.

LIBERALS FEEL SUPERIOR

They think they're better than us. Their superiority drips from every word/gesture and it sux.

OVERCOME THE HERD

Sometimes one can only resolve perplexity and sadness by music/a view as we reminisce.

When little tiny boys are seen as future oppressors you know there'll be female abuse somewhere.

We all do what we do, that's all. Some sing, some dance, some just think and many fall.

LIMERENCE

When self-worth's undermined it's the basis for limerence, which is obsession with persons.

Conditioned to get self-worth from others, trauma brings the immediate seeking of complementors.

The idealization of the romantic interest gives them the temporary validation they crave first.

The projected superiority of the narcissist gives a sense of comfort/love from early rejection.

Manipulations mirror the dynamics of her childhood so encourage limerence [infatuated].

The familiarity of even violence can provide comfort if it mirrors what she knew in her childhood.

Abuse forms strong trauma bonds between abuser and victim esp. with happy-sad vacillations.

ARE YOU LIMERENCED?

The unpredictability of such dyads creates a heightened emotional state: to INFATUATE.

His come here-go away style creates the emotional state leading to limerence--it frustrates.

OVERCOME THE HERD

The victim's brain is wired to associate the highs and lows of abuse with love and excitement.

For victims, limerence can temporarily fill the void of low self-worth or fragmented identity still.

The intense focus on the limerent object allows the victim to escape pain by validating herself.

Like any addict, anything to get temporary acceptance and love even though it is based on illusion.

You may not have a man rocking your world right now but you're not miserable like you were gal.

People make me laugh. They either take themselves too seriously or miss the important things see.

People make me laugh. They either take themselves too seriously or miss the raw, TRUE reality.

THEIR ATTACKS ARE BUMMERS

Attacks are bummers. "What all said about you was right and I shoulda married your brother."

He gives you a taste of the imagined future reality but there's strings attached/forgotten quickly.

Breadcrumbers are preying on your hopes and dreams for the future: just give now/he'll pay later.

They use future faking and your real need for validation to lock you investments into them.

If all you did was lose at slot machine, you'd leave. There's gotta be wins to keep you cleaved.

Watching how narcissists manage conflicts is a measure of psych health: it's a volatile hell.

OVERCOME THE HERD

They use future faking and your real need for validation to lock your investments into them.

They seem so nice/even tempered until conflict occurs and **THEN** you see how they are immature.

Sudden unraveling reveals haughtiness and nasty anger. They are depressed down under.

On edge: Your one wrong comment away from their irritability--like a grenade range, truly.

One wrong comment and they aren't slightly annoyed, it's **BOOM** as it all comes out--what a guy.

THE CONFIDENT NARC IS FRAGILE

The strong, confident narcissist is actually fragile. You're walking on eggs to keep him stable.

To avoid such **FALLOUT** we learn to avoid many subjects, we get weaselly and it's like a hex.

We can't talk about this nor disagree with that--can't even make distinctions without his crap.

It's so taxing to engage with a narcissist I advise you to keep your cool and disengage when pissed.

When you get defensive he now attacks that and it's on to the races with you an anxious doormat.

Being a receiver of narcissistic disregulation will make you a madwoman: you don't need him.

They gather data on you to trot out when it's time to **WOUND** you to maintain control he's got.

You cease to exist. You filter **YOUR** reality through him and that's the codependency with narcissists.

OVERCOME THE HERD

Finally, you lose self in the relationship and feel you cannot exist without being in their grip.

Fighting doesn't work, he wins. Leaving doesn't, pulled back in. Fawning works, like when children.

Don't run old grudges & events thru your mind, it only makes grooves. STOP this, I behoove.

THE CURE IS GRATITUDE

The cure for depression/complaining is gratitude. God said "never forget what I've done for you".

Truth tellers are ostracized and punished in the family for seeing what they see: that was me.

Never forget the narrow escapes and His rescues from people's hate. God is good, remember ok.

Self-doubt, perfectionism, anxiety, depression: these result from a childhood in chaos son.

We walk around with bleeding wounds and don't know it. Codependency & need to please shows it.

A need to edit oneself, being in a fog concerned with other people not our inward volatile hell.

In the muddled home mess we lose concern for self, it's everyone else while we're an empty shell.

Result: being pushed around, unable to set boundaries, afraid to ask for a decent salary.

BREADCRUMB RELATIONSHIPS

The tired victim settles for breadcrumb relationships, insincere friends and Jezebels splits.

OVERCOME THE HERD

A shitty life can indicate a loss of self issue. It's always there but covered over by falsehoods too.

But we can heal those wounds from a break between the true self and our daily charade.

If one comes from a dysfunctional home, boundaries are not respected & borrowing is expected.

Violation of physical space: your brother is taking your clothes and bringing friends to impose.

REFUGEES FROM DYSFUNCTION

The upkeep of the false self takes incredible energy and THAT'S why he's so mean and prickly.

He doesn't care about your things. He grew up in a home where all combined everything.

Powerful women/intense artists have self-control lest rage takes em over the cliff or to hell.

Powerful women lose power [to control circumstances] by succumbing to crutches.

The absolute grief of being constantly undermined has to be overcome--by taking control hon'.

Once the victim sees she CAN control an impossible situation by going no-contact, she's won.

Instead of going no-contact the weaselly woman holds on tighter, creating more abuse than ever.

TAKE CONTROL FOR TRUE SELF

Take control and decide for the True Self: Never be compromised again by an emotional hell.

OVERCOME THE HERD

Never postpone recovery & feeling good. You already know you can't go on with this hood.

Now it doesn't matter what he does cuz you severed the situation like you never knew the scuzz.

By going no contact your thoughts will eventually fall in line. Be easy on yourself/avoid that swine.

WE ARE BORN SOVEREIGN

We're all born sovereign but also born into a system which awaits us and demands we conform.

It's the end of our country. Without borders we're not unique, just one among many but/w money.

Tyrants desire the foreigners for one reason: they are far easier to control. Aristotle

The habit of tyrants is never like anyone dignified or independent, since only they are that. Aristotle

To be romanced and unveil beauty in a great adventure—that's what makes women come alive sir.

Woke is Maoism with American characteristics. CRT calls everything racist until they control it.

Woke is Marxism attacking the West. We cannot cure it until we understand it's not just a pest.

NOT ABOUT RACISM BUT POWER

It's not about racism but power. "We don't care if a cat is black or white as long as it catches mice."

One week was UK coronation and the next week was the end of our nation thru mass migration.

OVERCOME THE HERD

The news: I didn't vote the left so why should I have to suffer hearing about all the devastating effects?

The "people" are those supporting communism, the "enemy" are those against murdering millions.

THE END

Every word or action you make should reflect the highest life you can conceptualize ok.

Solution: focus on self and other relationships. This allows edging out while getting a grip.

Instead of experiencing many things superficially it's best to slow down: take less in but deeply.

Just cuz all our high school friends are dead doesn't mean we're next. Remember that instead.

THE HERD IN US

DREAM ON AS YOU LEAVE CHAOS BEHIND
ENERGY TURNED DESTRUCTIVE
MAKE LUCAS MCCAIN YOUR DAD
DON'T LET EM IN/GET INVOLVED
IT'S A ROUGH ROAD
HIPPIES HATE FLAMBOYANT BEAUTY
TDS ACROSS THE LAND IN WOMEN
BUILDING SELF-AWARENESS ALONE
HEALTHY SHOCKS ABOUT PEOPLE
MAGNIFICENT ENERGY AND SUCCESS
SNAKE VS. HEALER EMPATH ARCHETYPE
BREAKFAST ONLY PLAN FOR SAINTS
DAILY HEALING OF GERD
FASTING IS THE HIGHEST HEALER
STARCH IS THE STAFF
HIGH CALORIES TO LOOK AMAZING
FATAL MENTAL DISORDER
ENDGAME THOUGHTS
THE NEW WORLD RENOWNED YOU

THE HERD IN US

DREAM ON AS YOU LEAVE CHAOS BEHIND

It's **OK** to dream of mansions in your future. But hippies hate that, even our thoughts are censored.

In just one incident I learned this man would hurt me inadvertently/would be constant treachery.

SEE THE SIGNS and don't get involved. It's an adulterous generation the bible talks about.

After my healing he said **ONE** thing reflecting worlds of dark meaning and I was gone instantly.

Just to be cute he gambled with your relationship and about this kinda shit he learned quick.

You gotta see signs and symbols not take things at face value or assume too much: wake up now.

You're like a child now, super-sensitive and tender. To stay this way keep that barrier sister.

ENERGY TURNED DESTRUCTIVE

So you went wrong, who hasn't? So you were the worst, that's just a sign of your magnificence.

The exalted are born with most energy, which is more energy to sin when in the wrong direction.

For energy can go either way: creative self-expression or creative self-destruction/hell to pay.

I'm gone and I don't have to explain. Be like a cat who gets the hell away from toxic invasions.

THE HERD IN US

You're now a mature multi-level visionary genius recognized across the world as righteous.

The rich tend to have a galaxy of flatterers not gainsayers and this can easily implode sir.

Don't worry the gossip will dwindle/become less meaningful and they'll only see YOU.

MAKE LUCAS MCCAIN YOUR DAD

I If fatherless make Lucas McCain your dad. You can do this you know/imagination works fast.

People are cruel: I leave you with that. Always establish barriers or life turns bad fast.

He's not a genius: he's an unrealized, would-be genius who is now making an ass of himself.

We made it outa hell and living in heaven now. You can change reality too, just by decision.

DON'T LET EM IN/GET INVOLVED

Give them access to you and it gives them a chance to insult you. Speak but avoid parties fool.

Don't get in their car or let em in your house. Never be vulnerable should they suddenly change sis.

Our whole problem is anachronistic complacency. It isn't the fifties/things have changed drastically.

It's not what he feels today, it's what he'll feel tomorrow and the day or years after that honey.

I knew nothing as a foolish girl and in came the world til I was nothing and sought all the cures.

THE HERD IN US

A small desert town was my first encounter with Dunning Kruger: adapting to the dumber.

Hard to enjoy Christmas when everything's so preposterous like what they're telling us.

Just cuz they're catty and cruel the blame's not to be put on you, you're just a trigger or cue.

Spiritually it's important we be in the right place not where angels fear to tread: be home instead.

IT'S A ROUGH ROAD

It was a rough road having to learn it all on my own. Trial and error is a painful way to grow.

If you didn't learn it from parents you gotta learn it the hard way: the lower rungs are humiliating.

Him and his tribe: they all died. Divine wrath is swift for every one resisting you or who lied.

God is my Champion and Vindicator. He said vengeance was his not mine [it's way more].

Dream of living in Palm Beach if you want to, it's ok. Uplevel your sights, seek high end/pay.

They hate Trump out of jealousy and his love of high end EXPENSIVE things, that's the hippies.

Stick with elites and no more care what "they" think: losers and fools from the dark past see.

Hippies call everything beautiful "conspicuous consumption": it is budding communism.

Nothing more disheartening then a queen on the begging end from consciousness broken.

THE HERD IN US

Donald, the hippies hate you for your love of RICH, opulent beauty and operatic extravagance.

The old mansions of bygone eras in America were far more extravagant than Trump, it is God.

HIPPIES HATE FLAMBOYANT BEAUTY

Communist architecture is ugly and austere. Hippies hate flamboyant detail meant to inspire.

To operate with God in the highest creativity synchronicity you must be in solitude see.

I just wanna be alone/he just wants to be alone so it's a perfect marriage protecting our home.

Donald: Ye was presumptuous and silly in your office. That was an imposition on you the best.

Melania Trump: "I'd never chase a man who didn't love me, it is a disgrace". That's a queen ok.

Let Melania be your model and stop chasing the rabble just cuz it's easy on a tablet/get a life.

Having relocated and free of PTSD you feel God's power flowing freely as success attracts to thee.

For what they put you through [and Donald Trump] was evil, corrupt and nearly destroyed you too.

TDS ACROSS THE LAND IN WOMEN

Marriages split across the land between Trumpster husbands and wives who despise "him".

Have a healthy fear of people. Dig in/gear up: lay boundaries and enforce barriers against evil.

THE HERD IN US

Wives: "Trump is the most despicable human being" and they hate their husbands liking him.

TDS is common with women and yet none can explain why: like most females it's socially driven.

Things were never better than under Daddy Trump yet females hate him like the envious/dumb.

"I'll give her one more chance and if she says something I don't like again, that's it" said the twit.

Filthy sins reflect in the muddy aura of mauve tones, not quite clean clothes and dirty fingernails.

BUILDING SELF-AWARENESS ALONE

A lack of self-awareness prevails when one is wrapped up in cycles of addiction and fails.

When God was done with a certain area He took you out and those who remain can't recall it now.

I sensed destiny as my past had been but a preparation for this trial. Winston Churchill, WWII

Your most fruitful hours are spent doing nothing. God gives blueprints in these blissful times.

Should you read this or watch that, or should you just look out the window to get God's plan?

Had a list of ten videos to watch today but looking out window is more important I heard God say.

Went to a Palm Beach party and it blew my mind. A little store on corner sold caviar, oh my!

Went to a tiny store in Palm Beach and a valet took my car. I could get used to this as a star.

THE HERD IN US

So his kids have mansions too, so what. Envy/hate is never easy to deal with-- it's a block.

It is far more profitable to look out the window and dream not cave to dregs/trouble see.

Don't ask WHY a friend's gone just open to the next one coming around as doors close then open.

HEALTHY SHOCKS ABOUT PEOPLE

I was interested in a dashing man but something he did shocked me and I never saw him again.

If he so casually does things that hurt you now, do you really think you can change him at all?

Even if you "caught" him thru sex, how would you keep his interest? You gotta think long term sis.

Ok so you caught him, how you gonna keep him? There's nothing deep here sister, amen?

Melania would NEVER chase a man. She would be disgusted at the thought in her mansion.

She dreams of snaring that clown thru sex: it's a massive soul tie but she can't see this.

Meat is a luxury when things get rough. Live on starch and add produce: gather not hunt.

MAGNIFICENT ENERGY AND SUCCESS

That magnificent energy is about to burst forth sparking divine revolution as things change course.

That magnificent energy is about to have mass appeal as God lifts the veil: be ready now/kneel.

THE HERD IN US

You can be so stoked on someone and suddenly see him, the devil inside making you sick man.

SNAKE VS. HEALER EMPATH ARCHETYPE

He's a **SNAKE**: a serpent, a master manipulator and charlatan--don't let him in and begin again.

Don't get in their car. A frenemy drives you on errands but only takes you on toxic detours.

You will be sorry if you let him into your house. You're a sitting duck being so dumb, get hep sis.

So it's an archetype you're playing--don't take advantage of that with the laity, be godly.

You've chosen a high archetype and it's a sin to take advantage of that like many/MANY have.

It's just an act while here on earth, a strata of expertise or worldview and a high accomplishment.

I do have friends but mankind in general? Uh-uh, it's a cruel animal. Holocaust survivor

Show up at the WH with military uniform and a smile, walk out with fifty billion smackers, aye.

BREAKFAST ONLY PLAN FOR SAINTS

You only eat once a day then may have to rest see. It's ok its only once then have **FULL** energy.

In higher echelons obesity isn't an option. I'm that way too, I understand and solved the problem.

Not nutrient density but Satiety Power [foods taking you longer] since fasting is the highest healer.

THE HERD IN US

Breakfast only plan for the saints: You're high all day and every moment is cornucopia ok.

The breakfast only plan cures all middle age dowdiness and keeps you on top as well as fitness.

Eat whatever and how much you want, enjoy thyself. Make it a happy time of day, breakfast.

French toast/pancakes/omelettes/bacon/pastries all go thru, colon's mass evacuation holds true.

Fastarian consciousness takes hold [alights] in the afternoon as transit time completes too.

If you do eat you'll see you're not as happy and the results are not as nifty-- learn that way.

DAILY HEALING OF GERD

Daily fasting: the only way to heal Gerd symptoms of belching, bubbles and acid pain even from water.

I have that and dare not stir it up. Not even water in the aft: let digestive rest and love to fast.

Fasting managed human interactions while eating brought cycles of despair/frustration.

Daily fasting: I'm on top of things while they're down in the gut digesting: divine fighting.

Without the knowledge and boldness to express this they'd throw you in an E.D. clinic fast.

They won't let em daily fast or omad [One Meal a Day] in E.D. clinics, it's three meals conformists.

E.D. clinics: dystopian authoritarian hierarchies enforcing strict obedience not independence.

THE HERD IN US

Give me just breakfast--a big one--in the Ed clinic then I'll fast. Would they allow that? Never sis.

It's amazing how filling shortbread is darling--it's far better than meat/petite like a little lady.

It's ok to be skinny, in fact you should be for maximum longevity. Give body a break from heavy.

FASTING IS THE HIGHEST HEALER

It's far more important to fast after breakfast than any benefit derived from two more meals sis.

Pastries every two days is fine for me. Life is now incredibly simple and I'm never hungry.

Careful Melania, you were thinner before. Fast after breakfast and see I'm right/it's better.

Gonna speak from Palm Beach and tell em how to keep skinny and sweet by me, a seer so deep.

Eating once a day is superior and you can go two days here and there: how easy it is to star.

Each continent on the earth has a dominant starch it can live on should things get austere.

Corn, spuds, rice, wheat: each continent lives on starch when things get rough--learn from that/see.

STARCH IS THE STAFF

STARCH is our **STAFF** to live on, to keep from perishing when things get rough, to plan on.

It was a Fatal Mental Disorder but the world doesn't care, in it's eyes you were Satan's whore.

THE HERD IN US

A fatal mental order and queen's disease in a world taking her under/breaking her down see.

So you gained five pounds, maybe you're best there. Get outa the numbers game/be happier.

Pastries, powders, piece cheese: what is more nutritious and rational for the satisfied/skinny.

With butter on the donut it's like a time release capsule each moment with full satiety: love it.

HIGH CALORIES TO LOOK AMAZING

Add calories to your pastry by melted butter see then you'll look amazing before the fasting.

The maximum hair dress is coconut oil or animal with water. This make it like glowing steel sir.

Eat something simple/available/offered to you. It's only once a day and heck, it all goes through.

I like to finish my meal with piece cheese, after my butter-soaked broiled twister donuts see.

I drink lotsa water with my salty/tasty/oily meal but not later, it's a dry fast for 24 hours or until.

It's not so much **WHAT** you eat as it is how much you fast later after whatever you ate.

FATAL MENTAL DISORDER

A fatal [want to die] mental disorder of queens sick of being invaded and made into slaves see.

Are you not happier/look better on a radical early carb punch then no lunch? That's you hunch.

THE HERD IN US

If weight goes down or up a little, let things settle. Cease seeing only numbers and smile.

As you are happier and things improve psychologically so too the body, your true weight honey.

I too weighed constantly, an obsession. It's the same with age: forget numbers/enjoy creation.

ENDGAME THOUGHTS

You need some rest I heard God say. How about just thought and music today? I said OK!

So you're an endless spout, you need SOME rest, do you not? Please God make it stop.

Just when you decide to take a vacation out pours new inspiration. A writer is being on-call hon'.

TDS Trump Derangement Syndrome is such a stupid thing especially when in your own home.

Should I get to work? No honey, music is more productive today and every other time see.

You have shown yourselves to be exemplary and God bless that see as rewards accrue today.

A flash in the pan and then you're gone. Don't worry, that's the way it is--just have fun.

The place to go is Iowa, the exact center of America. See the truly valuable, not the coasts fella.

THE NEW WORLD RENOWNED YOU

As the past breaks down like a dream a whole new vista opens and our genotype genius alights see.

THE HERD IN US

The world will look at you and see a realized human being, a light in the dark, a divine thing.

I'm an endless spout since I got the devil out. What a trip, clean and free, pure and humbled.

Come with me, let us enjoy this higher reality together. It's a cornucopia after enduring whatever.

THE HERD IN WORDS

BORN CLEAR, WE MAL-ADAPT TO OTHERS
FALSE KINGS COLLUDE TO BRING US DOWN
WIDE PATH TO HELL
GROWTH FROM TRAUMA
ALCOHOL ALLERGY
SELF-MEDICATING HIDDEN TRAUMA
FOOD ADDICTION AND BULIMIA
FEMALE GUARDS THE WORST TORTURERS
THANK YOUR ENEMIES
LECHERS ARE TEACHERS
TOXIC SHAME IS PUT *ON* US
WHY THE NECESSITY OF NO-CONTACT?
ENTERING A LION'S DEN
LESSONS WHEN YOUNG AND STRONG
ELDERING AND OLD AGE
RELOCATION IS ESSENTIAL
TRAUMA AND THE CHANGED BRAIN
CHANGED FOREVER AND CLEVER
THE VALUE OF NO CONTACT
THE SEASONS ALWAYS CHANGE
ELDER CONSCIOUSNESS IS THE APEX
TRAUMA BONDING
VESSEL FOR GOOD OR BAD
WE COPY ARCHETYPES
COMMUNITY IS TYRANNY
VACILLATION IS THE SIGN
ARCHITECTURE FOLLOWS CULTURE
NO FORTLIKE MANSIONS FOR ME
GO TO SAFE AREAS AND NOW
LONELY RECLUSE FIGHTS EM OFF
INTERMITTENT REINFORCEMENT
DO YOUR WORK, WAIT TO BE DISCOVERED

THE HERD IN WORDS

TURN IT ALL OFF: IT'S AN INNER JOURNEY
LET EM GO: IT'S GOD YOU SHOULD KNOW
YOU'RE AT THE TOP OF YOUR GAME
INDEPENDENCE: IMPORTANT. SOCIAL: NOT AT ALL!
CONQUERED BY LIBERALISM
AT FIRST THEY'RE YOUR FRIEND
THE WICKED BLOCK YOUR WORK
GENIUS LOVES LEISURE AS A TREASURE
WOMEN DEBASED
PUNISHMENT POSTPONED
JUST STAY HOME!
STABBED IN THE BACK THEN SUCCESS
GOD'S FAVOR AND HOLY SPIRIT EASE
STRESS RELIEF IS THE HIGHEST
NEVER BORED OR LONELY AGAIN
NO WASTED YEARS
BULLIES OSTRACIZE
COME OUT FROM AMONGST THEM
THE PAST IS ERASED!
USELESS PURSUITS DELAYS GOD'S GIFT
TREACHEROUS FRIENDS NEVER AGAIN
HIGH BOUNDARIES: NEED A FENCE!
LIFE STAGES: ARE YOU READY?
WAIT FOR INSIGHT, DON'T FORCE IT
FIND YOUR TRUE REALITY
BACK DOWN, REGROUP
LIFE'S A PARADOX: MISSING THOSE YOU SHOULD BLOCK
RELEASE THE OUTER FOR G OOOD
PROGRESS FAST: RESTORE OLD PATHS
NEVER AVOID BITTER TRUTH
GLOBALISM VS FASTING
WHAT YOU'RE ESCAPING:

FRENEMIES
PEOPLE HOLD US DOWN

BORN CLEAR, WE MAL-ADAPT TO OTHERS

Born clear we mal-adapt to an insane world and the smartest get the sickest or they find the pearl.

It's the price you pay to be a star. People can raise you up but will also pull you down, so beware.

Those favored by God are hated by man. They hate your success so don't try to explain, just ban.

Having someone tyrannize over you is the best education to be a good leader.

Our God is so good--He gives reprieves till the very end. No matter how sick or failed we can still win.

It is the fact I could never please them that I got so good cuz it compelled constant improvement.

If insecurity compels constant improvement then maybe that's God's plan but eventually let it go, man.

Dark night of the soul: Daily tears, God's curse: used to educate us and prepare for battle of course.

Your trials give you something to say. Now they'll really hate as God turns your ashes into a bouquet.

Your troubles gave you soul--making you warm, empathic and glowing while the others remained cold.

A new season, a new day: power and prosperity, all pains to allay. It's called "blessed"--enjoy God's buffet.

THE HERD IN WORDS

FALSE KINGS COLLUDE TO BRING US DOWN

People are cruel, they keep you down. Haters gotta hate something, it keeps their blood flowin'

The human python is Social Hypnotism and it's all we've known in human society from the beginning.

They believed Hitler and so they turned on their neighbor. Social hypnotism: that's culture.

I've brought sibling abuse to light but there's so many other things like this: hidden/minimized.

False kings collude together against God's men and women. Expect it: smear campaigns, gossipin'.

WIDE PATH TO HELL

In the latter days it's a wide path to hell and it's like everyone's an empty shell under a spell.

Cell phones increase social hypnotism exponentially. Think of the pets left out of the mazeway.

What of "trauma"? You have a roof over your head and food to eat, no trauma. Holocaust Survivor

They loved me quite a bit, of course it was traumatizing when they suddenly treated me like shit.

Mean coldness brought personality devastation. He became wormy, weasely, cowardly, cowering.

Holocaust survivors never talked about it, aye. If they dared to they'd be crying all day and night.

GROWTH FROM TRAUMA

When suddenly thrown into a concentration camp those children tended to grow up very fast.

THE HERD IN WORDS

Fast growth: prison, concentration camp, military, sudden crises or separation into godliness.

Fear of loneliness or people-pleasing behaviors are solved by solitude in the wilderness dude.

Suddenly I was put in a group who hated me. What a growth challenge to find solutions/the key.

Challenging environments increase intelligence cuz it's a matter of survival just to happily exist.

I had supreme audacity but after a group incident I lost this tendency and became far more savvy.

From interactional synchrony [humming] to dys-synchrony [grating]: now destiny's fading.

TWO separate nervous systems, not just one. Shifting gears, all creativity died and I was done.

Called right or left, trophotropic vs. ergotropic or other binaries, let's just call it dark or happy.

I switched to the left with alcohol/drugs or bad food, habits or associations all taking me down.

So you learn how to maintain the high: it's from walls, boundaries and assertion defenses, aye.

I just wanna get up in the morning and be high all day and night working--that's from separating.

It took me ten years to get him to give me office hours without interrupting which he did eventually.

ALCOHOL ALLERGY

To drink means anosognosia: all loss of pattern recognition and making an ass of myself again.

THE HERD IN WORDS

Anosognosia, a chemical switch to the left: you are killing yourself without ability to see it yet.

To drink means a hangover waking up terrified of impending doom. Never again this gloom.

The terrifying hangover is an allergic reaction to the worst legal poison of history/civilization.

The mere ATOM of alcohol causes anosognosia so even cough medicine or Nyquil will do it to ya'.

Killing yourself without the ability to see you're killing yourself: who needs this, be a happy elf.

It took two days of chemical injury to finally return to my pink cloud of happy childlike creativity.

Sometimes I think of a cold beer on a hot day but then I work it thru in mind to the HELL I'll pay.

Just to show the binary, I'm a sweet lady but with alcohol become a harridan, worst in history.

SELF-MEDICATING HIDDEN TRAUMA

Didn't know how to handle trauma and emotions as a youth so sunk in my swill with alcohol too.

I had no boundaries so alcohol soothed the hurt from being controlled, being swallowed whole.

Was so immature if a store clerk was rude I'd have to get drunk to adapt to extreme pain/inner feud.

Alcohol brought up inner demons called "ego alien" and it was frightening to others in the system.

Multiple Chemical Sensitivity [MCS] made alcohol benders a catastrophe physically see.

THE HERD IN WORDS

Alcohol didn't work so I switched to food to handle my ocean of emotion of psychotic devastation.

I was always happy when I was eating, then only happy when I was eating. Now I'm happy fasting.

FOOD ADDICTION AND BULIMIA

Food addiction is progressive just like alcohol. That's why they get to be 600 lbs like a cow.

Bulimia won't solve this dilemma czu then it's that demon called an ugly green thing of millenia.

If one with MCS gets fat they can't breathe so the only answer is to eat ONE meal then fast for lean.

Having survived addictions I am rarely hungry, one meal does me beautifully and I never drink surely.

Bulimics sink to a lower level and begin doing other bad things like kleptomania or slutsville.

Bulimia facebook groups won't talk about ancillary behaviors because they have blinders.

To survive PTSD realize the old life [miserable] was the opposite to the new one [quite wonderful].

FEMALE GUARDS THE WORST TORTURERS

The female guards in the camps enjoyed their power immensely, just as Geo Soros said recently.

In retrospect the women said it was the best time of their life deciding who lives and who dies.

It makes perfect sense that the craving of the powerless would be for total power over life and death.

THE HERD IN WORDS

In like fashion, those who've been victims become the best leaders later knowing what it's like hon'

Either she gains empathy by being a victim or goes the other way and enjoys torturing like scum.

Ok so you went thru a few horrendous things in order to learn and grow. Please, **GET OVER IT NOW.**

Compare your situation to those in the holocaust and agree you've nothing to complain about.

THANK YOUR ENEMIES

See life as a ladder and PTSD ceases to matter. Back then/down there was your bootcamp instructor.

Ok so he scared you, pushed you in a pool, wrecked your rep at school--now you're a better girl.

I'm so much better and well-boundaried cuz you invaded me constantly and made me nuts/crazy.

I have such a better understanding of myself after you invaded and put me in your stinking hell.

I know my limits so much better after you busted all boundaries and then degraded me further.

LECHERS ARE TEACHERS

You were my best teacher being such a lecher. I never knew men could be that bad you poser.

Just the fact you were in that situation indicates you needed defenses against it so forget it.

The farmer's young sons loved their power. All they had to do was put a swastika on their collar.

THE HERD IN WORDS

When they hate you they hate you and can do anything they friggin' want to you: that's people.

Young thugs scout neighborhoods enforcing Nazi justice: when it comes to grudges people love this.

They all did it. Not just get something cheap but take over your shop, flat or all your savings see.

They will justify anything they want to do to you if they hate you and I mean polite society too.

Sorry to pop your new age bubble about loving people but God should come first not part evil.

Someone important to you leaves town never to be seen again. Man is ephemeral, God is eternal.

Soros said he was never so happy as when he was ruining Jewish lives. It's human nature, yikes.

When there's a pack of wolves you howl with the wolves. When they steal you do too I guess.

You were loved, now you're attacked. Where things were happy/smooth they're now hostile/rude.

Scary as hell, adapting to ups & downs of human nature. The smartest go into solitude I wager.

Love, security, kindness, blessing. Those are the feelings when it all turns around again.

TOXIC SHAME IS PUT ON US

She murdered my rep, I killed the bitch back--by living a destiny and improving every day in fact.

They put toxic shame on us to deflect from them the culprits. We only sinned to cope with this.

THE HERD IN WORDS

It's their toxic shame cuza how they think from someone else's game, put on you the innocent ok?

Get this straight: this shame you feel day and night was put ON you by the malicious and the snide.

Be a shame-buster, a shame-rejector or anything you wanna call it to release mental prisoners.

If you did something wrong you feel shame, repent and forget it--but this is input from the wicked.

It's the shocking awareness that they wanna harm you and make you miserable--your own folks.

And when a whole family/town feels there's something to feel shamed about they create castouts.

This isn't about category or identity but human reaction to novelty--a godly uniqueness in everybody.

If genius has a propensity for the arts and the others are noncreative/fat hearts, he's their target.

Joyce Meyer raped 200 times by age 10 by dad. The message? Success is possible no matter what.

A new neighbor can ruin your life so you gotta move out. That's why I bought all adjacent lots.

From wimpy scared black sheep scapegoat to lightning rod enlightening em to start creating.

WHY THE NECESSITY OF NO-CONTACT?

Why no contact? Cuz there's something in their DNA that wants to hurt/hate/cause harm, alarm!

If you're afraid of someone you don't let em in, you alert the neighbors and call 911, you hear friend?

THE HERD IN WORDS

They may not even know they cause harm but all we know is they DO and we're DONE, adieu.

If I'm gonna lose my identity around you with your mean projections why bother shrew.

It may seem a small thing but the implications of not doing it are life-shattering, see this please.

ENTERING A LION'S DEN

No way was I prepared for the lion's den I entered. I was unaware of social hypnotic patterns.

We're conservatives. We're not into burning cities down or smear campaigns, we just want home.

Almost dead I get the fruits of my labor, perfection, a few bucks in the bank and mass attraction.

When young I had to be strong enough to endure all those lessons getting me to here, huh.

Now I love solitude, order, naps, doing my own thing every moment, no adapting whatsoever.

LESSONS WHEN YOUNG AND STRONG

I could never endure those lessons today. They were scary, draining, terrifying, waste of pain.

So why have PTSD over those painful lessons, they got you to here didn't they? Success, fun.

If your parents can't teach you then the world will and it will be FAR more humiliating and painful.

What I learned the hard way: Never let em in lest you know em & NEVER get in a car with em.

THE HERD IN WORDS

Live a life of isolation cuz it's far more fun, an inner journey of excitement and adventure hon'

The less involvement the better off you are. That's the way it is as with atomization/computers.

You'll reach a point of being so good you'll automatically be in the limelight so don't rush that.

ELDERING AND OLD AGE

Start taking leisure seriously. The would-be genius has an incapacity for leisure so he fails surely.

Picasso and Frank Lloyd Wright were at their highest apex in their nineties then died suddenly.

In normal aging you don't get sicker you reach your crescendo as a worker then die in an hour.

Can't believe you dumped him here ok. You know I love privacy but you take advantage anyway.

Even the blameless concentration camp survivors felt guilt and shame, it's how abuse works.

Guilt, shame, a feeling of unworthiness, can't get up again, giving up into sin, addictions, dying.

RELOCATION IS ESSENTIAL

Satan is a python snake that wraps itself around you till you can't breathe, think, feel, move/relocate.

Relocation is the go-to device always, the bottom line rule: just extract yourself from fools.

We swim in muddy waters so we get stuff on us but it recedes with maturity then we just forget it.

THE HERD IN WORDS

I kept company with demons and didn't even know it till I grew up but still I'm accountable for it.

Gotta relocate--it's the go-to rule. Society is obdurate once you've been pegged with smear tools.

Relocate, start brand new life that very day. Stay and be ridiculed, mocked and smeared ok.

Stop apologizing to dead relatives, just do it once. Same with prayer or it becomes a chant.

When Loves Raymond got canned laughter it wasn't funny any more & words didn't matter.

Don't ever use Holocaust comparisons, they're always false. Don't EVER do that, get some class.

And to all you Holocaust deniers out there, who are always leftist liberals, go to hell.

TRAUMA AND THE CHANGED BRAIN

You don't need "closure". Just get up and close the door, you'll feel much better when it's over.

Toxic shame enmeshed in cellular memory--imagine that, it's all through us blocking victory.

Trauma results in a changed brain. It's proven by pictures you'll never be the same again.

It's abandonment that creates trauma and it's coming home to yourself that gets you out of it.

After going thru that you're hypervigilant--street smart: perfectly adapted for new life to start.

Call it nurturing your inner child or reconnecting to the true self, prepare for the amazing results.

THE HERD IN WORDS

I'll always be hypervigilant having learned my lessons but lets change the brain again by relaxin'

I'll never be that naive girl again but also not that cat in a room full of rocking chairs.

CHANGED FOREVER AND CLEVER

All the dis-eases coming from my trauma: chemical sensitivities, hypochondriacal tendencies.

Fear of the future, shame over the past: I try to stay centered in this moment, a party blast.

They're dead or in a rest home. There's no vindication or closure on your part, just call on God.

They did wrong, we've done wrong. Forgiveness is about everyone and things even in the end.

If Joyce Meyer can forgive dad for 200 rapes by age ten we can surely forgive anything too friend.

Transform yourself from inside out first from education on trauma then affirmations of higher self.

Shame is internalized when abandoned, losing the authentic self & ceasing to exist psychologically.

THE VALUE OF NO CONTACT

NO CONTACT also means to his channel don't go back. A complete blackout, you don't know the chap.

A lot of people abandoned Donald Trump. They were reluctant to sign up but now've come back.

Suddenly we were just ships passing in the night, a vain imagination, a gut ache and sore delight.

THE HERD IN WORDS

Just like that, you're onto a brand new life. In a twinkling of an eye, just one insight and no more strife.

It's actually the devil luring you back in so you must go no-cotnact and that means on EVERYTHING.

Suddenly I transcended the dude. He meant nothing to me, I was elated with the end of this feud.

Nothing feels so good as going beyond a problem. It's a whole new vista opening up: relaxation.

Wait a little while and you'll see that problem resolve. Either disappear from mind or death/a fall.

THE SEASONS ALWAYS CHANGE

I sense the seasons changing. Onto a new cycle of destiny, God and liberty, I'm anticipating.

The Lord said: to the extent men have used you/spit you out you'll now be celebrated by them a lot.

I had a wonderful life. Whether cabin or mansion it was immense enjoyment and pertinent learnin'

But I was vulnerable to abuse. Out in the wilderness without a wall--as I look back it was obtuse.

I've done my work as God said to do it and tho' I'm always adding to it it's largely done and it's good.

I immensely enjoyed a tiny cabin on 1000 acres without a car. I learned to love it and it changed me dear.

When I had learned what I was there to learn God took me to a pretty mansion with cozy protection.

Trauma is trauma whether it was from momma or subsequent abusers who triggered it.

THE HERD IN WORDS

People are the worst addiction of all. We inherit attractions to styles that are well, hell.

Well all I want now is peace, tranquility and order to maintain my days. A place for creativity.

ELDER CONSCIOUSNESS IS THE APEX

For I am a human and humans evolve thru stages and I wanna experience the elder thing/sages.

I can sense your spirit, I'm not dense. I'm glad you're interested for it's all about our new success.

My insane behavior was a mal-adaptation to your liberalism but I accept responsibility son.

That ordinary citizens become mass murderers overnight and justify it--social psychology explains it.

If you don't heed your parents you have to learn lessons the hard way as the world does it IT'S way.

It took decades to recover from PTSD from the trauma with you but It wasn't just that, it was momma too.

Perfect strangers taught me the hard way cuz I wouldn't head mom/dad but now I learned it anyway.

Body is torn down from psychic attacks from sisters, brothers, lovers, whatever--disease takes over.

You misjudged me for years and when everyone bought it I had had it and my nervous system gave up.

Now I have a heavenly Father and Jesus is my brother and I keep these central, no family dramas.

God punishes sin. When He does it is terrible as His wrath is terrifying let alone publicly humiliating.

THE HERD IN WORDS

I would stay on His good side if I were you. Don't take a chance of falling, His rewards are sure/SOON.

TRAUMA BONDING

I didn't love him until he rejected me. Attachment trauma was triggered and then it's all about mommy.

It's not only unnecessary but a bit superfluous. You should stay quintessential: just you for us.

When men used women it was always for "it" and it's so dam hard to forget this humiliating event.

I don't wanna have that degrading thing on my mind! That's what it's all about, staying refined.

Cuz then your speech is contaminated with this crap--that whole level comes thru not your map.

People talking about their genitals--it's unreal! Personal things too, all from what is taught in schools.

Ever study WWII? That's how they did it: thru public ignominy, soul murder, rep-killing, CALUMNY.

It's so hard forgetting this humiliating event! All from what's taught in schools/what men should expect.

You should watch your speech. Cuz what you're doing in private is coming through, so I beseech...

VESSEL FOR GOOD OR BAD

What I do is directed by God at this point so guess He's using me now for you, if for only this minute.

I love being a vessel doing footwork for the Lord. Only in purity is He using me and I love it/I ADORE.

THE HERD IN WORDS

I planted the seed and what happens now is not my responsibility. I'm a thinker/planter of theory.

I accepted the unacceptable--then everything reversed with me on top again like long ago.

Acceptance reached brings reversal. You avoid it all your life then when you finally do it you're all new.

The answer is to be happy for the success of your enemy. Believe me it's coals on his head /you're free.

They can't stand how we love our cats. Let this be your barometer: go no-contact with a man like that.

You must treat it thusly: They're dying to get in here, every minute you must watch cautiously.

Not only am I fenced up I'm in a safe state. Arizona Strip is more like Utah than AZ--conservative/free.

WE COPY ARCHETYPES

I wasn't so much being sinful as I was copying an archetype thrown out there by evil people.

"Maybe this isn't such a good idea. Maybe I should go". What happened after that, do you know?

All grandma in a rest home says is "are you the slut?" cuz she doesn't remember anything else, duh.

All people recall is the ARCHETYPE evoked not the person nor behavior particularly--just the type.

You mean be part of your stable? Hell no! Your whole life is about that as far as I can tell.

And if you're NOT interested, fruit you--cuz I'm interested in myself and if you can't see it I'll say adieu.

THE HERD IN WORDS

No, the narcissists tendency is to trigger jealousy, a rudder for control but it chases me away.

COMMUNITY IS TYRANNY

I couldn't believe the setup in Borrego Springs where it's all community not individuals = TYRANNY.

I know you think you can do it thru a mystic environment but that's false--if in sin it'll bite you in the butt.

After the lovebombing phase they're cruel, condescending/find things wrong with you.

Once the devalue/discard starts it can feel confusing cuz up to that point they were madly lovebombing.

The devaluation can be strong or subtle but in either case it triggers in the victim a desire to fix it all.

The loveboming phase is FUN but the discard phase is no-fun as your heart and soul is ripped out.

It starts subtle—a remark about your hair or dress: playful teasing then ends in projection/GASLIGHTING.

The nitpick and this point or blame shift for things they run to quick. An emotional maelstrom, sick.

It's well worth it to get the image of a married woman whether or not you get along with him.

Suddenly there's a personality shift as Jeckyl becomes Hyde. You can't predict it but what a ride.

VACILLATION IS THE SIGN

No matter how nice a guy seems if he love-bombs then discards he's just another narcissist freak.

THE HERD IN WORDS

He seemed so understanding like the perfect empathic man but then he pulls the rug out suddenly.

He was handsome at 16 voted most likely to succeed but looked like a cartoon when I saw him at 50.

It's in all the ancient war manuals: At times the superior man must lay low. Wait for it but stay humble.

I had to stay low for years in a small town. If I ever got too big they'd slap me down. It's the women.

This was part of my journey. Learning to put breaks on strength--the true definition of "patience".

They didn't know anything about me and I had to lay low without identity just to avoid problems see.

ARCHITECTURE FOLLOWS CULTURE

It is fascinating how architecture follows culture. Homes in high-crime areas are like windowless forts.

There's no view windows in suburban forts in high-crime areas but beautiful floors, kitchens etc.

Why are you in a high crime area anyway? I can feel it one hour away, can't get far enough into country.

Mexican architecture isn't just artistic but functional for high-crime areas. Thick walls and window slits.

These mansion-forts cost a mil but is it worth it living like this, with high crime reflected in the mental?

Mexican architecture: It's a beautiful thing and rational but I'd rather be where it's low-crime still.

You would never see those fort-like structures where I live, where everything is normal Americana.

THE HERD IN WORDS

These fort-like mansions are plentiful in Mexico but now our Southwest and I was surprised/chilled.

Southern AZ is violent and we're talking gangs all around who invade the suburbs too. Not for me/you.

NO FORTLIKE MANSIONS FOR ME

The safest place in America is Southern Utah/Northern Arizona, confirmed in Strategic Relocation.

The peace I feel when everyone around is normal and into their own homes and I never see them.

It's hard to feel safe in a high-crime area just cuz you're walled in. But for many of you it happens.

It's beautiful when there's ironwork everywhere but then the nervous mind says "why is it necessary?"

It helps to know that incessant, nagging guilt and shame is a result of Complex PTSD: repeated trauma.

I've done my work and I've suffered. Now I couldn't bloody care less, it's all about my home sir.

My home is practically all windows as the scenery is revealed everywhere-- that's a low-crime area.

Slits for windows--never thought I'd see this in the United States with these architectural changes.

From daily porch talks/visits to SLITS for windows and never even knowing your neighbors: changes.

GO TO SAFE AREAS AND NOW

There are safe areas. You don't have to live like this--slits for windows and always looking around ya.

THE HERD IN WORDS

They don't like the crime but CNN lulls them into complacency and being inward-grown.

Ironwork and walls are very beautiful but firstly they're functional at keeping the herd out ya know.

We are changing speedily demographically, socially and architecturally and it's tragic but fascinating.

Staying low/putting brakes on strength [patience] was at a later date my rocket launcher into space.

They didn't know a thing about me. I had to socially adapt without triggering their response to novelty.

Their response to novelty in social generations could be to kill me. It happens in the gangs freely.

I was terrified knowing I could not make them understand what I am plus the burden of just being woman.

The solution was marriage then getting the hell outa liberal California into a conservative area.

In a liberal social town I had a big bull's eye painted on me. Liberals are violent towards any novelty.

Ray saved my life from a liberal town. He immediately legitimized me so they'd leave me alone.

That was 14 years ago and it's been UP UP UP from there. I just needed protection to thrive and flower.

Ray kept people away and asked them to leave! Without him they'd just keep coming/imposing on me.

LONELY RECLUSE FIGHTS EM OFF

It may seem strange that such a lonely person would fight off people trying to get to them. Hmmmm...

THE HERD IN WORDS

I felt the older women wanted to kill me, at least psychically and socially. They were really ugly.

To KILL my reputation: CALUMNY, soul murder. God'll get em for this later, don't worry my sisters.

I was visited by the angry church ladies who wanted to force me go to their boring socials or else.

The church socials weren't just boring they were MEAN and it's an undercurrent I don't really need.

Not just boring and mean but an UNDERTOW: Wouldn't I be SO MUCH happier just in my own home?

So goodbye, I've loved you all my life but God has said "enough--he's just a cartoon now, a lie".

People start out handsome/pretty but as they absorb the lie they become caricatures of humans, yukky.

The handsome specimens are men who fought wars, seated in true reality not just some fantasy.

Men who fought wars know what life is all about and don't complain about childish, petty, silly things.

Men who fought wars, women who bore and raised children to be Christians. Reality not liberalism.

Look up "78 year old men" and you see disaster on their faces save one the veteran who looks amazing.

Liberals get ugly cuza what they believe in like abortion in America. There's no way out, it's looks karma.

It's not that war-fighting is good but it reveals true reality not the disasters from living in fantasy.

INTERMITTENT REINFORCEMENT

THE HERD IN WORDS

Narcissistic relationships are based on intermittent reinforcement: sometimes bad, sometimes good.

With time the positive reinforcement becomes more spaced out with more negative filling in.

They want you, they get you, they push you away onto the same old abuser track--sometimes in a minute.

Trauma bonding: being loyal to someone who is destroying/actively working against you.

These relationships all start with many amazing promises so we return to them without any real evidence.

It's trauma bonding that keeps us stuck. The ups and downs are like heroine when the foe is back.

DO YOUR WORK, WAIT TO BE DISCOVERED

Just do your work then wait to be discovered. Only God knows the day or hour but you'll get the power.

I'm in the groove man, the predestined thing planned before my birth: I'm in the flow, synchronicity now.

Reason to be sweet, gentle, loving and self-controlled: it saves energy.

It's your time so resume dreaming. Keep that dream alive: no need for scheming, God is redeeming.

Fill it with each other = becomes an echo chamber. Fill it with God =continuous revelations so clever.

You worked and waited, now it happens overnight. In the twinkling of an eye, success out of sight.

You don't need a gift to preach or sing. What gives you power is affliction--then a giant upswing.

TURN IT ALL OFF: IT'S AN INNER JOURNEY

THE HERD IN WORDS

Turn off all shows--it's most important to get into your own thing now.

We sin to avoid anxiety but then anxiety gets worse, triggering us to sin again--that's how it works.

A point is reached when seared conscience melts down. A period of tears follows then the Self is found.

In elder years the temporal lobes open up to reveal eternity: panoramic perception in a smaller body.

It's not that you created a higher reality, it's that you repented and God gave it to you mightily.

To make a dent in society we must be famous--that's obvious--but can we handle it? Must do it.

After much suffering I asked God for help and He brought me back with a Creative Act--done, in fact.

FALLEN HERO SYNDROME

In the fallen hero syndrome, boundaries dissolve and evil worlds flow in to the end of you/your home.

Dark night of the soul is over. What a curse but I learned so much and now it's time for takeover.

Since the greatest saints were the worst sinners the best future can spring from the worst past.

What made Jesus' speech powerful was word pictures and that's also true of Einstein/all discoverers.

I just want someone who's neat and nice--is there anyone left like that or is it way too much to ask?

They must adapt to you or you'll never get anything done. You're problem is being eclipsed by them!

THE HERD IN WORDS

How could I know my foes were my friends--it was always them that was "loving and good" they said.

LET EM GO: IT'S GOD YOU SHOULD KNOW

Let em go, people aren't important. It's God, He's first and foremost--men move, die or go dormant.

Kellockialisms are brutal logic reversals

It's hard to get her out of her home even if she's moving up higher because it's what she's known.

I know we get busy but don't forget to party cuz the incapacity for leisure blocks genius or the arty.

Can't rush ahead and force it myself. I've learned that from false starts, humiliating failures/God Himself.

I've done my work, it's complete. But am I going to market myself? Never, all problems He'll meet.

Be an exemplar in your generation. That's opposite to them--it takes strength not to slide down.

Yes he's the king of narcissism/egotism but we love it cuz God designed self it's like a magic elf.

If your motives are good you can be as arrogant/conceited as you please, just not a cheat/sleaze.

Like pooh on the shoe it keeps coming back so why we need a desktop Manual to keep us on track.

You're at the top of your game and it's outstanding, electric, cosmic, the apex--cuz you gotta fence.

YOU'RE AT THE TOP OF YOUR GAME

Be yourself, incredible as usual. Style, magnetism, nerve, wit, grace and boldly/bluntly unstoppable.

THE HERD IN WORDS

Style is nothing you can fake--you're born with it. You either have it/not and when pretended it's rot.

I wanna build this airplane not get dragged into neighborhood politics and that's what's cosmic.

If you've a right to be mad, then squelching it will only bring stress, mental illness, disease/bad.

If you don't even have a sense of order you're clearly of the devil joker.

He was a hick from the beginning and you thought you could change him.

Don't worry over enemies when you see em again old age got em.

Accept all delays as the fastest route.

I told you not to work, you did anyway so God took your computer away.

Music hypnotizes pets so I can work.

Party for three days, blow it out. Think of green pastures, mellow out.

Anti-depressants for just two weeks caused mental illness for thirty years-- rages, divorces, tears.

How could it be that someone so entirely brilliant could get so messed up--the worst of the lot?

I hope you enjoy this journey through my mind. If you don't, kindly drop me and I'll attract my own kind.

If you think all those selfies are interesting you've got another thing comin'. Do something not just shovin'

INDEPENDENCE: IMPORTANT. SOCIAL: NOT AT ALL!

When I wanna work doesn't conform to time or place so that means no social for the ace.

THE HERD IN WORDS

Don't let anything--not one thing--track your mind. Now let it all come up from deep inside.

When God wants your own thing all else is static but since you've been tracked, you're still on it.

Insist on your right to sit/do nothing but look out the window. Meditation is most important dumbo.

Don't let em tell you how to do it. Do it your way though it makes no sense, just the way you intuit.

You gotta catch crap when it happens. Nail it, something's wrong, use instinct hon'

Your project like the Taj Mahal: Attention to detail, incredible intricacy and beauty, intense focus.

The rest of the world is really creepy. Even the Europeans are liberals, letting em all in/a tragedy.

Because I relaxed, by refusing to work, I got the insight that collapsed the whole mess into a lark.

Think I'll refuse to work another day, relaxation is so profitable and enriching, ok?

CONQUERED BY LIBERALISM

We had it so good, we were different in a rare experiment that worked until conquered by swine.

We had it so good, our men were decent. But we were debased into immorality four decades recent.

The barometer of barbarians is how they treat dogs and that's most of the world: want Americana!

Most of the world is really creepy but we were different.

Now the SJW starts up about how terrible America is.

THE HERD IN WORDS

Self-selling women really turn me off. Let it stand on it's own, boss.

If you use your art to virtue signal on trendy topics you're not an artist. For art is eternal not this bull.

I don't virtue signal on trendy topics, I'm trying to undo all this.

Maslow said the superior man has only a few friends his whole life, so get a life.

AT FIRST THEY'RE YOUR FRIEND

First they're your friend then compete with you in front of others--sign to drop em (false brothers).

If something doesn't add up, if it's stuck in your craw, if you can't get over it: bring it up, look at it.

If you sense exclusion or triangulation (two against one) see it as important and let it be central, hon'

Don't let things go by, you'll only stuff or smoke it down. Face it, discuss it, keep the day flowin'

The contagion of madness is such that we've made each other sick. Work on mixed signals, think.

Victimized, she became mentally ill in that system. Stockholm Syndrome: she took *donations* for him.

Their hate is a sign God's getting ready to bless you. So don't justify or explain, just bid them adieu.

Just by being yourself you unify all opposites. Refuse all categories and live your separate life.

THE WICKED BLOCK YOUR WORK

Assembly of the wicked enclosed me, wild dogs surround me, a gang of evil men crowd around me.

THE HERD IN WORDS

They always hate you to begin with and can't wait to stab you in the back as soon as possible. True?

Put that whole bad era in a bag/throw it out.

Greatest suffering = greatest poetry. Relaxation = greatest creativity.

Just be in the groove: be a supple paint brush in God's hand, I behoove.

Relax and let God and the angels take the reins now. You've done the work so now recede, go low.

You've checked to make sure it's all right. Now send it so all doors can open with God's might.

You were just the vessel for the Creative Act. Now that you've given birth, enjoy the fruits/just relax.

Having birthed the Creative Act you're also mature, it's the same path.

Insofar as you come to God you come to the True Self. For those talents were designed before birth.

If you've checked it, just send it. Now party until the benefits.

You plant a seed, you WAIT, you reap the harvest. It's not immediate--the waiting part is a must.

You did it. You went against the grain, you went with your instincts, you fought for privacy to do it.

It's not yours anymore, it belongs to the world. You were just the vessel for this magnificent work/wonder.

People of principal do what they say they will do and never lie. Compare that to today and cry.

You've done your work now you can be a child again. Just like Jesus said and it's the right brain.

GENIUS LOVES LEISURE AS A TREASURE

THE HERD IN WORDS

Take a day just for music, no left brain linearity. Now you'll feel an absolute torrent of creativity.

I'm done now I can just have fun.

There's a spirit of strife. She's cold to me but she's your friend so what is going on, I don't like.

It's all erased: that's the miracle of Jesus.

Dear Lord please cleanse my memory. That's all we have and it can ruin one's whole life, believe me.

If you can't afford a house with a fence, rent a cabin in the wilderness. Solitude, escape the mess.

I was hurt not by him but the Wife of the Alcoholic Syndrome--after first drink anything can happen.

WOMEN DEBASED

Women debased, hated/baited, called ugly/berated, scapegoated: became queens or didn't make it.

I became a queen through all that. No one has higher boundaries than this comfy house cat.

There's one in every town, a slut. She's been so invaded by men her low self-esteem seeks em again.

They call it "slut shaming" as if it's a good thing deserving of respect and dignity (also ok: obesity).

We must be more vocal. Our problem is complacency cuz we want our own privacy but it's not-ok.

People have spirits. With the first contact their influence can conquer and make us feel non-legit.

I went through the Wife of the Alcoholic Syndrome just to write about it. Research it, then forget it.

THE HERD IN WORDS

Especially if the male alcoholic has all the power OMG this war will get very bad, Satan vs. God.

PUNISHMENT POSTPONED

You can commit evil and go on for a long time--but sooner or later God's gonna cut you down, swine.

I'm already fulfilled by who I am. I don't need fast cars, a bigger home, a jet-- just to defeat bedlam.

With changed mind about a person, we hold the inconvenience he causes us against him. Nietzsche

Way to success and happiness: Don't think about the past or peoples.

Don't be crippled with remorse over what devil did thru you when weak--Jesus erased it if you believe.

We've lost the millennials but not Generation Z. These are the teens who are Trumpists and serious.

She tried to tell me what to do, to superiorize over me. I finally blocked the witch, who is she?

Transition makes you need Him--it moves us into prayer. Thus it's followed with success, so prepare.

Success is greater than all your suffering. For every tear you're stronger, no need for bluffing.

JUST STAY HOME!

Loneliness teaches how to be a leader. It makes you tight with God--no need to "fit" or be a breeder.

Home is so important to us it's the first thing one loses in war--and in disaster, the greatest crisis.

THE HERD IN WORDS

I told my husband I'm just gonna stay home and never leave again. You take the cars, have fun.

They were much worse in the 80's insisting you go out--like it was a sin to be happy as a lark.

They called me ungodly cuz I didn't wanna go to their church parties--like it meant I didn't love Jesus?

Home is where all my things are, a perfect set up, my pups, my family and God is the loving Host.

Let em bark, they'll learn you can't adapt to them and find something else to do or chew.

Now just think of success--of crossing that great divide between total enchantment and this mess.

GET BETTER THRU REST

You can only get better resting. Conserve strength until your time has come with God's blessing.

You have already done more than enough. To just casually take the crown you need to rest.

The minute you explain yourself they lose respect and start to test.

You left me alone but your memory makes me better, not a clone. Thanks for putting me on the throne.

With God all things are possible. Always remember that lest in down times you become irascible.

The great are lonely. The more significance to what they built the more they must watch for phonies.

It's getting ready to overtake you (what you've been crying for): success--real progress, largesse.

THE HERD IN WORDS

Before you're blessed you're hated. We go through "pain on purpose" but it's just a test--your success is fated.

STABBED IN THE BACK THEN SUCCESS

Anytime you're stabbed in the back but keep on walking, God's set you apart for success—blessed.

You don't wanna be my friend? It's okay, I'll be all right because I'm never alone: on God I'll depend.

She's a diva but she's got diva neurosis. She has no lines, too edgy and does immature interviews sis.

After it's over you'll see why you went through it. It's all part of the bigger picture and God always knew it.

About Sparky: If he thinks you don't love him anymore (because you discipline) he starts barking.

Repentance: the stairway to heaven, the only way to right-brain living where it all fits without leaven.

You know how bad it is, but still God loves so now just enjoy thy day and stay sweet as doves.

There are always problems and fears but I know Jesus lives and loves me so I will persevere.

GOD'S FAVOR AND HOLY SPIRIT EASE

When God gives favor He makes your enemies bless you. Though they smeared, now you're revered.

The very fact you went through all that (and are still here) is a sign you've been assigned, a gold mine.

My best friend and uncle died. Now I'm filled with power as words flow out, as if supplied.

THE HERD IN WORDS

That a few mere words could find success and fame, without selfies and pictures everywhere?

I didn't play silly games or compromise to get here. I just overcame being stabbed in the back, then a seer.

STRESS RELIEF IS THE HIGHEST

It can be done. Knowing this relieves stress and life becomes fun. Know it-- and new life has begun.

If they don't want you, they're the foe--a non-issue, a John Doe. You've had it up to here, you know?

Relax to get the insight, blocked with tension.

It's best to just sit, look out the window, listen to music, toke and up comes the phrase or joke.

The best creativity-releaser: start the weekend on Tuesday.

On the weekends you are released from petty details and trivia. Saturday is purely right brained.

You want to drill down to the insight you need. That only comes from relaxation then it's freed.

Keep untracking the brain. Music is best, a movie tracks you in a groove no matter how great.

Empty the brain. You got too much static in there. Free it, look to eternity, let it go, be rare.

Men are always comparing (she knows that) so when he looks and looks her reality goes splat.

The fact we're getting all the pedophiles and bringing back God, He still may change His mind.

Maybe you're afraid to go deep. Forgive yourself for everything as Jesus erases it all/NOW see.

THE HERD IN WORDS

God changes His mind about punitive actions with repentance: Return from the brink/confess.

NEVER BORED OR LONELY AGAIN

Your creative action is your destiny so if it's not right or if helpers mess up it hurts, it's a blight.

Cut-off gestures: closure. I was so upset I lost all composure until the end brought on my future.

It's best to give em a funeral. If they've disowned you, disown them back: this is particularly crucial.

With death all problems are resolved. Everything we thought was important, isn't: in thin air it's dissolved.

She was the kingpin of the system setup so when she passed, trouble let up.

Poets all feel pain, many die of drink or fear–unless they know Jesus, then they just persevere.

If they don't want you, let them go. More often then not it's because you're in-the-know or they're the foe.

Since the biggest obstruction is people, eliminating them will bring ecstasy as out goes all evil.

It was a Cinderella System of two against one (me) so when one passed the system dissolved (free).

There was a hellish time they had power over me and now I see they were for Hillary.

They ask you your age so they can peg you and feel superior. Don't take a chance, never tell em.

Even when I was 30 my great aunt said NEVER tell em your age. She knew it's an ageist society, ok?

THE HERD IN WORDS

Even my husband said block that guy who asked you your age. Remember it always to stay a sage.

COME OUT FROM AMONGST THEM

You're the best/they're a bunch of bores.

Don't be ashamed at the extreme proportions sin took: for that is it's way, a serpent mistook.

Democrats across the nation are revealed as corrupt and vile criminals as Donald Trump continues.

Women see antidepressants as happy pills but two weeks worth can destroy 30 years/even kill.

Say what you want about founders (for all men are sinners)--the constitution is a winner.

Without her there the entire system with other abusers dispersed--I don't think of them now, the worst.

Push these people out of mind, they don't belong there. Keep it only sweet and kind with lots of prayer.

Focus on one thing and you've blocked other things. It's like a budget, so let go and your heart sings.

You must disown back to keep your psychology intact then heal from all their group attacks.

So much to worry about--about this there is no doubt. The cure is faith and prayer until fear is a drought.

As a poet emotions use few words. It's as deep as the ocean when discussing God's rewards or curse.

If you're empty, don't work. You're a creative artist, not a clerk. You gotta wait for your quirk to get the perk.

Remove the deadline and outflows the Creative Act. This proves how important

THE HERD IN WORDS

it is to relax.

If one's conscience isn't seared, he just "knows" things. But the cold are dense/have flings.

Repent and shoot up like a rocket. Sin was obstruction (even gossip) but now God fills your pocket.

I'm so sick of old hippies who say they're "loving" but go for wicked things like homos and baby-killing.

THE PAST IS ERASED!

God turned things around for job after he prayed for his friends. It works great, like a cleanse.

RX: Transform your mind: Stop all you're doing and mentally transport to another place and time.

People who judge you by your past don't belong in your present. So true--reject, or be soooo blue.

With Jesus the past is erased---but not with so-called friends who will bring it up in your face.

Through Jesus sins are literally erased and that's called the "absurdity" of the gospel--seems impossible.

Turn em all off and get back into music. The repercussions of not doing so can be tragic.

All needed insights from looking out the window: By allowing your mind tracked you just stay in limbo.

You get to the point where you either survive or scatter. Man up: focus only on that which matters.

On treacherous friends: never speak to them again. Champions insist on absolute fidelity, amen.

THE HERD IN WORDS

God sees truth but waits (while we gain patience building strength) before storming the gates.

After cutting off all outer that tracks, keep the mind usable by God--let music/nature evoke facts.

USELESS PURSUITS DELAYS GOD'S GIFT

Don't delay God's gift with useless pursuits! Don't fill time, maximize it--by finding your spiritual roots.

Don't call it addiction but a neuropathway--a compulsive robotic groove. But cut it loose anyway, I behoove.

Turn it off and focus! Let nothing track the mind, it's hocus-pocus. Do your own thing--that's the locus.

God has a plan: Your blueprint destiny, a whole life span. If it's hidden from view, just repent to find it, man.

You don't have to say one word. Once you know something your vibration alone changes your world.

Finally, after years of scattered forces it all came together in a rod of power: the man or woman of the hour.

Just think of God and you're always home. He's in every corner making it clean and shiny as chrome.

Keep your mind supple. When dense, get out of the bubble. Don't get hung up or it's trouble, double!

TREACHEROUS FRIENDS NEVER AGAIN

Cut it loose and you snap to your goals. Since it was obstruction now your whole destiny unfolds.

When caught up in ego all creativity stops. This is when the brilliant voice becomes a wet mop.

THE HERD IN WORDS

Say it simply so there's no doubt what you mean. They've got A.D.D. and are hypnotized by fiends.

Sin warps creative energy. Give up sin = release of talents and gusto to act: breakthrough!

You have to achieve a certain level of audacity. It's boldness and it's from repentance (no mendacity).

You get to where you're so sick of em you transform and it's a divine battleship protected from swarms.

Must learn the Art of Walking Away Gently. No big thing just cut it loose while shooting up mentally.

NO WASTED YEARS

Forgive yourself for wasted years: the decades of dung when you knew nothing but sin and your fears.

Repent and sin vaporizes into thin air. Redemption is instantaneous--for God is most clever.

We don't think thoughts we choose those going by. It's totally your choice to be sad or stay high.

Be like a door: Let nothing in your thoughts, body or home that obstructs—then soon less becomes more.

Use words penuriously: no superfluity or non-essentiality. This frees up time-- no needless complexity.

Obsessing over movie stars is like looking at the dirt. Noticing the stars above Is fascination--now stay alert.

I'd do anything to get away from the crowd. I took the dive in '85 and ever since been alone with God.

Sometimes I gotta shut it all out. Start all over, bare bones: just music and thought, rid of the rot.

THE HERD IN WORDS

One time you did not react and you've won the pot of gold. Smash neuropathways and be bold.

Eliminate TV and a whole other universe illuminates: Turn the lesser off and infinity compensates.

Cut it loose (people, habit, food) to re-focus on eternity. Wipe the slate clean to optimize ability.

To rid remorse for past sins, mentally put them all into a bag. Now throw it out: because of Jesus you've a right to brag.

Your own talk show will just occur. You don't have to do a thing but grow then have your own chauffeur.

We love our small dogs. They're everything to us, ever-attendant as our nurturing instinct's triggered by God.

BULLIES OSTRACIZE

Bullies ostracize: they size you up and cut you down to size. If shunned your soul dies but in solitude it revives.

After aimless years he came alive, focused (on his best) then came to the front from the rears to his crest.

Purity = perfection and protection. It's not a random stew but what we do that determines God's predilection.

You could look inside the person to find the reason but I look at the system where hearts are freezin'.

They get so mad they swear. That's where they go wrong, without a prayer. You must stay pure to take the boss chair.

Sin draws fire but repentance is total protection. It's simple: look not outward but inside for affection.

Hate turns to love but also love turns to hate. Don't pile it on for things break when at hell's gate.

THE HERD IN WORDS

You've already done your time. Remember that to expect good not bad: just stay in line and be kind.

If those guys on stage don't talk about the police state--kills us/takes our stuff--what good are they?

HIGH BOUNDARIES: NEED A FENCE!

I didn't need a therapist I needed a locked gate and high fence.

They're cajoled to cross that line and once they do all hell breaks loose, that's how the brain works.

Demons take worse forms in each generation: it's dis-eugenics, or bloodline degeneration.

Know what it's like to be invaded by inferior characters: the necessity of high boundaries/markers.

Of course they act stupid/silly cuz they're all in sin or condone it in friends.

The creative act matures underground and is unrecognizable until that moment of completion/elation.

Goal: to replenish the sources keeping me creative. K.D.. Lang

It's not about status symbols but staying productive and creative.

If you're always alone the cultural mud won't get on you. Take it as a complement with gratitude.

Excruciatingly deep emotions expressed through a nugget, a pearl, a story, a concept, a two-liner.

It's not the majority rules when it comes to religion and we're becoming a minority fools so start fishin'.

My husband and I couldn't be more different: that's the birds and the bees but that's what pleases.

THE HERD IN WORDS

The superior man is marked by his need for solitude. Being separate is holy while they are crude.

What if the people you're trying to impress our now dead? You thank em for the incentive to be best.

We all have a niche we have to find and I found mine: Fewest words have greatest impact if it rhymes.

I went to the school of hard knocks and it was transforming. You gotta do this or you'll be conforming.

The greater the task the more Satan triggers weaknesses. Overcome (make gold) and the result is human genius.

Just substitute pages, no corrections please. No one can do my work I gotta do it *JUST SO,* that's me.

You've done enough: stop action. The ball's rolling in your favor, you can't stop it, need relaxation.

LIFE STAGES: ARE YOU READY?

It'll be easy now. Holy spirit ease--but only if you relax in leisure.

What you went through was horrible and humiliating but now you'll have the perks for all the trouble/waiting.

Finish you work, let 'er fly--see what God has to make you high.

Poetry is the science is least words.

False prophets declare their own works. True prophets works speak for themselves. Mat. 7:22; 9:25-26

I pray the work of your hands will make an amazing new dent in culture or turn the ship around for sure.

Life stages of a person: starts unrefined then ends a true genius with a Creative Act of the rare kind.

THE HERD IN WORDS

Now the end occurs: completing old cycles and beginning new ones. Glide through the transition, it's fun.

Some people prefer a separate reality being alone with God and pets. They're not the herd but the eccentrics.

Clear the decks so God can give you what you want. You're blocked with distractions, that's my rant.

No TV--It's priming us for bad things in a diabolical plan, you see? Focus on your own home and family.

WAIT FOR INSIGHT, DON'T FORCE IT

Secret to best work: wait. The superior man never acts unless cued--that's what makes him great.

People who judge you by your past don't belong in your present. So true--reject, or be soooo blue.

You follow gurus and mentors until you mature. Then you sift and decide for yourself: boss chair.

What are you getting out of this? Meaning, acceptance--or just filling time while destiny is missed?

Must just show up. You've studied, cried, overcome those who lied--now just shine as you reply.

Hold back (strength) until your time has come. Then it's power unleashed (never called dumb).

"Lord, turn it around!" Repent and return from the brink like Nineveh--then feel bliss like nirvana.

Pneumaticity is "leaving a space" which can now fill in. The best way to work is to just start chillin'.

Fights are a case of wrong identity--you are misperceived and miscast as the enemy. Just be friendly, okay?

THE HERD IN WORDS

We frantically search the internet to avoid True Reality. But it wouldn't be if you'd just be open/let it be.

My favs are becoming boring to me. I'm sick of input: I want to create and from all outer chaos be free.

FIND YOUR TRUE REALITY

Search the net: what you're looking for isn't there. It's True Reality, but leave a space for prayer.

Friends and family may be on the other side. They refuse to face the truth so from you they hide.

Give 'em a break: use few words. They can't take it in (as they are the herd) so cut it down by 2/3.

Need to divorce the past? You'll be in a new cast. For you were miscast as fool for seeing so vast.

Get off the net. It's not helping, you're just procrastinating from true reality where your soul is, I'll bet.

Fact: The more social media, the less happy.

The only constant is change and the earth remains. Grace Jones

With God the worst day of your life can become the best.

You hurt and cry then everything turns around. Wait for this reversal and you're heaven-bound.

Divorce all snobs--you must. For they feel superior but for you it's self-esteem or bust (only friends you trust).

By snobs your identity is framed and it's a lowdown thing being thusly chained. Reject, esteem reclaimed.

Due to the era I grew up in I became a sinner but didn't realize it since the world called it a winner.

THE HERD IN WORDS

With the needed insight, don't do a thing on it. Sit on it, let it percolate--don't fret on it, now do it.

What to do when you see who he is: Don't get in a tiz for you knew it all along but stayed mind-fizzed.

It wasn't you being bad--you soaked it up like a sponge. That's how brainwashing makes us grunge.

He's the man giving me the life I love. That's reason enough to treat him well and be sweet as a dove.

For many life is in the pits. Don't let it continue--whatever you do, repent and shake the devil to bits.

BACK DOWN, REGROUP

Back down, don't push back. Now pray as God pours ashes on his head and his world turns black.

Women: don't push back but back down. For female power is silence then you wear the crown.

So you made a mistake. Just pray and watch God turn all-bad to all-good for those who have faith.

Compulsive behaviors are mental illnesses, even speaking loudly in public for attention is sickness.

Compulsive behaviors are from stress. Tho a form of PTSD they should still be addressed (no finesse).

Ever notice how the compulsive also gossip? It's put-downs compensating shame in the closet.

All behavior is compensatory, psychologists say. Look deeper than symptoms--were they betrayed?

You've done nothing wrong but there's a war on your mind. That's why you often feel down, or unrefined.

THE HERD IN WORDS

Every woman is wise and foolish, clever and absurd, good and bad. It's a package deal: good vs. cad.

If there's nothing coming through the spout, don't write. The worst thing is to force things--it won't be right.

There were times in history where people became crude. Picking their nose, pissing in the street, lewd.

I have a mental picture of the concept in time, a phrase comes through and then I finish it with a rhyme.

Most everything is PTSD. Otherwise we'd just be normal, you see? It's a matter of obstruction: debris.

Problems like anorexia and bulimia are post-trauma stress disorders: fear is a robot out-of-order.

What is the trauma? Involvement with wrong people forming templates of self-despair even for the able.

Borrego Springs is a beautiful desert island in a sea of sharks. Better to choose to live in other state parks.

You can't bring them up--they'll only bring you down. That's the reality of human systems vs. your crown.

LIFE'S A PARADOX: MISSING THOSE YOU SHOULD BLOCK

Life's a paradox! Like missing wrong people you should block: they seem like doves but are hawks.

Most all problems come from people involvement. Left to your own these irritations would be absent.

Be there for them as the veil falls from their eyes. When they see the light you'll hear the gullible's cries.

Go to bed tonight and wake up in heaven. Many people die in their sleep and what a way to freshen!

THE HERD IN WORDS

I write what I feel, couched in what I think. It's my way to deal with emotions while we approach the brink.

Those with most to say are shunned, ignored and minimized to their dismay. Wait, you'll have your day.

Popularity is no proof of the truth--but you gotta speak it anyway so the youth line up at your booth.

RELEASE THE OUTER FOR G OOOD

There's nothing on the outer anymore. Except for the view, it's the inner realm I'll glorify in and explore.

Dad didn't say it was easy but that it could be done. Now get off your butt, hon--and get disciplined, son.

They said it could be done, not that it was easy. People are sleazy and their wimpiness makes us crazy.

It's all just energy: dense vs. clear. The bio-drives (food/sex) become the most compulsive (no cheer).

For every sin there's a seed of compensation (punishment). God won't have to--it's inherent in the moment.

Take out the trash. Those people brought demons too and thus you feel bashed--now get back your dash.

In times of transition the archetypes explode. Take advantage of this opportunity to reach your goal.

Sin takes you down a rabbit hole of wrong decisions (no success) so the answer is to stay sinless.

Slow and easy wins the race. No sudden movements just daily diligence and it shows on the face.

To discern people, look at their track record. That's all you gotta do--not your heart (break that chord).

THE HERD IN WORDS

Everyone's the center of a universe and Facebook perpetuates this idea. Be creative: a genius galleria.

We started out right then got on the wrong track. How easy this happens in science or living in a shack.

They only care what benefits them. All other considerations are condemned-- they're not friends.

If wrong you'll always be proving yourself. We grow up by getting clear: putting it on the shelf.

To make progress restore old paths. They had wisdom and clarity, not like now when genius is a rarity.

PROGRESS FAST: RESTORE OLD PATHS

To progress fast, restore old paths. For they had power and class, unlike those acting like an ass.

If you're helping don't let em pile on other things too. You must draw that line, if you've a mind to.

God make me bigger than anything I fear. Though surrounded by the spear, put me in good cheer.

Ancestral ties bring great solace even in a dungeon, for courage and strength is their function.

The opposite to black boot tyranny is the beauty of nature--that's your therapy and God's your teacher.

We've fallen so far from the men/women of old. They overcame, they optimized, they found the gold.

See how fast you lose your currency with him. As ego's triggered he gets adversarial: foe not friend.

Return to the old paths--the only way out. It makes me sick what we're losing, all due to drought.

THE HERD IN WORDS

How to love when the other becomes adversarial too fast: This love story is no blast, being miscast.

In the past you'd fight it out, then you'd pout but now you're silent since you know what it's all about.

Watch out buddy, things can change fast and suddenly you have no control-- when you've lost your role.

You knew it before, just couldn't close that door. Queens know how fast things change, then it's war.

"The things he said to me used to make me truckle back in. But now I've got vision: his flip flops are sin."

NEVER AVOID BITTER TRUTH

The truth is seldom sweet, it is inevitably bitter. But unfortunately we must face that truth to get any better.

It hurts so much being physically objectified. It feels like being depersonalized, a nothing, soul-fried.

It should be irrelevant what you look like. Let your work stand on its own and seclude from the hype.

When it comes to breasts is bigger really better? To many it's a fetter-- inelegant even in a sweater.

Wisdom speaks when it has something to say. Fools speak cuz they gotta say something to feel okay.

She's devastated not because he called her fat but because he could be so cruel. Understand that, fool!

To be objectified hurts: it's scary to be not a person but just a number in the face of their flirts.

Suddenly you could lose all interest in me. That's what I mean about the lack of stability and fidelity.

THE HERD IN WORDS

Depression triples chances of dementia. Change your view: no matter what God rules minutiae.

GLOBALISM VS FASTING

Globalism is about a country's leaders selling out their own people and Joe Biden/sons are most evil.

Nobody is better at saying nothing than Obama. It's no message in a fantastic package. Adam Carolla

Jack Dorsey a billionaire fasts every day. That's my way of controlling weight loss and acid reflux ok.

It isn't normal aging it's what you're eating. You could keep youthful longevity but want the meat thing.

Your diet isn't right for you. Its bad effects are gnarly so I'll pray you change and stay away till you do.

WHAT YOU'RE ESCAPING:

Homeostasis: Being down brings pep-talks, being up brings insults. Thusly the system maintains itself.

100 KAREN KELLOCK BOOKS

AFFINITY OR MISERY
AGELESS CORNUCOPIA
AMERICA AWAKE!
AMERICA'S DAFT ERA
ARTS OF PALEO FASTING
AUTOPHAGY ON CHEATERS
BACKSTABBING NEUROTICS
BETRAYAL TRAUMA
BOOMERS AND BROKENNESS
BOOT ON NECK
CHAMPION GUIDES
COMMIE NUTHOUSE
COMMIES
COMMUNIST SPIRIT
CONTAGION OF MADNESS
CONTAGIOUS MADNESS
CULTURE CLASH BASHED
DAFT LEFT
DAILY FASTARIAN
DAM RATS
DIVERSITY IS CRUELTY
E-RACE WHITE
EVIL FREAKS (Beyond Gross)
THE END OR A BEND?
FEMALE BULLIES AND FEMI-NAZIS
FEMALE CARNALITY
FEMALE DUMB DOWN
FEMALE POWER DRIVE
FEMINISM AND RUIN 1 & 2
FIX FOR MISFITS
FOOLS & TRAMPS
FREEDOM SPEAKING
FRENEMY ENABLER
FRENEMY LIAR
FRENEMY THIEF
FRENEMY TRAITOR
TRENEMY TYRANT
GENIUS IS HELD DOWN
GLOBALISLAM
GOD USES THE FLAWED
HAZE OF THE LATTER DAYS

THE HERD IN WORDS
HIX POLITIX
HOW THEY RUINED US
JUST SKIP DINNER
LE FEMME AND THE COMMUNIST SPIRIT
LIBERAL CHAOS & ROT
LIBERAL DOUBLETHINK
LIBERAL GALL 1 & 2
LIBERAL SHOVE-DOWNS
LOCK YOUR GATE
LOSERS and Femme Fatales
MANUAL FOR SUPERIOR MEN
MODERN ART FROM HELL
MOSTLY FAKE
NOTES TO CHAMPS 1 & 2
OVERCOME FRENEMIES
PC MAKES US CRAZY
PEOPLE ARE CRUEL
PEOPLE PROBLEMS 1 & 2
PERSECUTED GENIUIS
POLI-PSYCH MYSTERIES
PRETENTIOUS SLOBS
QUEEN BEE
RED NEW DEAL
RETURNING TO FIRST NATURE
SEASON OF TREASON
SEPARATE MEANS HOLY
SOCIAL HYPNOTISM
SOLITUDE SOLUTION
SUPERCILIOUS
THE SCHOOLS SCREWED EM UP
TOAD TO PRINCE
TRIALS CYCLES
TRUMP VS. GROUP
TRUST IN TRASH
THE TRUTH ABOUT PEOPLE
UNDERHEANDEDLY CLEVER
WALK TALL WITHIN WALLS
WE'RE NOT ALL ONE
WINNERS SKIP DINNER
WORK OR SMERK

KAREN KELLOCK PH.D.

M.S. Political Science, San Diego State. Ph.D. in Psychology, University of California Irvine. Postdoctoral: UCI School of Medicine, Dept. of Psychiatry [NIMH Grants]. Developed the Debris Theory of Disease, a theory of system pathology in 120 books and 22 textbooks for the general public. The theory has a general formula: All disease is obstruction, all recovery is elimination, all success is attraction. The three obstructions are people, habit and food. Remove obstruction and snap to your goals, waiting in the wings.